IS BRITAIN GREAT?

THE CARAVAN GALLERY

IS BRITAIN GREAT?

FOREWORD

Joanne Bushnell
Director, αspex

The Caravan Gallery was established in the summer of 2000 when Jan Williams and Chris Teasdale converted a humble holiday home into a fully - fledged mobile gallery and took it on its first outing to the seafront at Southsea. Later in the same year αspex worked with The Caravan Gallery on the show *'About Yourself... an exhibition all about YOU'*, where the artists' obsession with the everyday lives and desires of the general public was evident. The work, a project about gathering, processing and displaying information, was only made possible with the participation of visitors and it is a continued engagement and fascination with people and the way they live that remains central to the artists' work.

During the last six years The Caravan Gallery has travelled the length and breath of the UK. Extensive periods of research - when Williams and Teasdale immerse themselves in the local culture, looking for what is special or distinctive about a place – precede appearances at locations to which they have usually, but not always, been invited. It is on these occasions, on the street, in the most public of places, when The Caravan Gallery successfully attracts and engages with the most diverse of audiences: not only the art cognoscenti, but also toddlers, 92 year old pensioners, nuns, drunks and dogs, to name but a few.

Both Portsmouth - based, αspex and The Caravan Gallery have developed a symbiotic relationship over many years. We could not consider opening on our new site without their involvement and are proud to work with Jan Williams and Chris Teasdale to present The Caravan Gallery's first major retrospective exhibition. '*Is Britain Great? The Caravan Gallery UK Tour*' is a highly subjective survey-cum-tour guide to the 'real' Britain in the new millennium. In an era when citizenship is taught in schools and we are all concerned with our local culture and environment, the artists invite us to question and consider the way we live today. Special thanks go to both Alistair Robinson and Rosemary Shirley for contributing engaging and perceptive essays to this publication, to Arts Council England, South East for supporting the project and to PPG Design and Print for sponsoring the show and for the provision of invaluable technical expertise.

The Caravan Gallery invite you to answer, *Is Britain Great?*

The Caravan Gallery invite you to answer, *Is Britain Great?*

THE CARAVAN GALLERY

Alistair Robinson

Alistair Robinson is Programme Director at
Northern Gallery for Contemporary Art, Sunderland

First published in 'The Condition of England' NGCA 2005

"England is the paradise of individuality, eccentricity, heresy, anomalies, hobbies, and humour."
– George Santayana, *Soliloquies on England*

Jan Williams and Chris Teasdale's photographs re-work the "rose-tinted tones of tourist information brochures" to create an alternative picture of national life. Williams and Teasdale's bittersweet records of their tours of the length and breadth of the country can make them appear more like a modern-day Daniel Defoe or Mass Observation than an advocate for travel, however. Their investigative appetite for observing our built environment, customs and rituals has generated an archive of several thousand images. Seen in series, their body of work constitutes a psychological profile of a nation entering a new century – or as they put it, "a highly subjective survey-cum-tour-guide to the 'real' England." The artists are drawn to both behavioural anomalies and curious juxtapositions in our environment. Many of the locations which the artists record are marginal rather than metropolitan – areas which corporate capital and civic 'regeneration' have either not touched or are just in the process of transforming.

Williams and Teasdale's individual images are threads of a larger canvas in which a story of our collective life is told, as if from the bottom up. As the artists note, "the very familiarity of our subject matter" can belie the complexity of their wider project. Whilst focussing on particular motifs in their repertoire can obscure, rather than illuminate the scope of their ambition, the artists are compulsively attracted to certain subjects. For example, Williams and Teasdale have a fascination with the ramshackle modifications and low-tech improvisations that we subject our dwellings and possessions to. They reveal not so much an alternative 'empire of signs' – although obscure, obscene and unkempt signage is a special interest – but an alternative view of how the world is layered. The places and objects in their world are frequently either amended or altered, improvised and makeshift, or otherwise being hastily rebranded and repackaged. Although such concerns draw to mind both Richard Wentworth's series *Making Do and Getting By* and Jeremy Deller and Alan Kane's *Folk Archive*, these facets of their practice are merely components of a bigger enterprise. As the artists note, their oeuvre is not only about "the celebration of overlooked details, where unexpected delights are to be found in the most unpromising situations". It is also about the fact that, as they point out, "the reverse is true."

The Victorian writer THS Scott, mapping the state of the nation roughly 125 years ago, opined that "the love of respectability and land are inveterate in our race." The title of his ambitious survey, *England: Her People, Polity and Pursuits*, could easily also describe Williams and Teasdale's project. Unsurprisingly, they are more interested in places which are unloved or underused; and in situations where the straight-laced stance of offering "approval of what is approved of", as John Betjeman put it, falls by the wayside. Many of their images are emblematic of peculiarly English inclinations towards irreverence and self-deprecation, and ribald, scatological humour. Profane humour, as the novelist Howard Jacobson has observed, is not only our most powerful intoxicant, but "gives us access to our other selves". In revealing the unbridgeable gap between our aspirations and achievements, we see ourselves, and our collective body politic afresh.

The artists also reflect the fact that humour is an inescapable part of English life. But it is, generally, a means to an end: they deploy it as a tool to engage our curiosity whilst offering harder questions about who we are becoming. As social anthropologist Kate Fox has noted, self-deprecation and irony are the defining characteristics of English conversation: "Humour suffuses the English consciousness. In other cultures, there is 'a time and a place' for humour; it is a special, separate kind of discourse. In England, there is always an undercurrent of humour. Humour is our 'default mode' – we cannot switch it off. Irony is endemic, a constant, a given, and is the dominant ingredient in English humour." Which kind of businessman, we wonder, runs the business cheerfully named 'Cupid Marital Aids Boutique'? ('Boutique', used as a suffix or prefix, has become a journalistic cliché to describe middle-class 'lifestyle choices', and so has an especially cruel appropriateness and inappropriateness here.) And what kind of clientele do they attract? And which of us would willingly retire to the 'new lifestyle' of a disused suburban petrol station?

As well as undertaking a photographic survey of the state of the nation, Williams and Teasdale also conduct questionnaires which consult the 'general public' about lifestyle trends and tastes. Characteristically, their choice of questions paraphrases and parodies academic anthropologists' and pollsters' lines of enquiry. One such survey undertaken in Portsmouth resulted in such dubious statistical findings as: '99% of people would rather die than arrange a pre-paid funeral'; '17% of people have won meat in a raffle'; '30% of people have seen their parents naked'; '18% of people avoid their neighbours when out shopping'; '57% of people manage to kill houseplants without even trying' and 'Alan Titchmarsh is loved and loathed in equal measure.' Each aspect of the artists' activities intertwines the topical and the absurd, the serious and the frivolous.

Despite many of their images beginning as comedy of errors, Williams and Teasdale's vision encompasses quotidian subject matter from the playful to the immiserating, the grave to the uproarious. The common denominator between their diverse focal points is that they are all, for different reasons, excluded from how we are shown to live, whether in media representations or in advertising. Our first response to a street of terraces in Leeds, for example, might be to recall the dramatisation of northern working-class life in films from Billy Liar to Billy Elliott. But a second glance reveals that this is an infinitely more complex, and densely coded picture of how the ties of co-operation and community are changed by and yet have survived through both dilapidation and gentrification. (In major cities, both telegraph wires as much as washing lines are a sight from the past.) At the same time, the geometric composition of intersecting vectors is one which Cartier-Bresson might be proud of. And street level, contrasting signals abound. Satellite dishes mingle with SUV's and estate agents' signs, as though the street were a stockbroker belt. The effects of 'enchanted wealth', in Carlyle's words, could scarcely be seen more vividly.

THE EXTRAORDINARY ORDINARY

Rosemary Shirley

The term everyday life is characterised by a number of ambivalent associations. On one hand everyday life is what is closest to us, it is banal, it is boring, it is what we are used to. However it could be considered that it is this very position of familiarity which means that everyday life can also be mysterious, exotic and strange. This idea seems contradictory, yet it is often those aspects of our existence which seem most 'everyday', which are ignored – taken as a given and therefore are passed by without examination. It is easy not to notice the things we see most often. This paradox of the everyday is evident in the work of The Caravan Gallery, who, through their photographs of the seemingly commonplace, reveal the exceptional within the everyday, the extraordinary ordinary.

Andrex and HobNobs in Cambridge

The shop window is resplendent, unlike the extravagant displays of luxury goods in department store windows. Here the look is achieved with the most meagre of household items: packs of loo rolls and washing powder. The lowly status of these objects, (they are "just" everyday) is elevated as their utilitarian value is replaced by a concentration on their formal qualities. A semi-symmetrical design based loosely on colour and shape has been built up, frustrated, one imagines, by requests from customers anxious to purchase loo rolls to match their bathrooms. Such requests lead to a packet of peach coloured Andrex having to fill in where a blue one should be. Arranged mantlepiece style, the top shelf is book-ended by empty lollipop containers, proof if proof were needed that this display is not about merchandising as much as aesthetics. An aesthetics which is not completely alien to the practices of artists such as Haim Steinbach or Jeff Koons.

Historically the phantasmagoria of shop window displays has been associated with modernity's influence on the everyday, revealing that commodities (even such ubiquitous ones as toilet paper) possess extraordinary properties and even the power to inspire desire. However from this image one is also drawn to speculate on the motivation of the shopkeeper, this gesture does not seem to stem from the purely commercial drives allied with high street shop displays. Here this aesthetic engagement seems to be generated by a certain pride in their work, the satisfaction of a job done well and above all an incessant (if perhaps slightly mad) cheerfulness which manifests itself in the elevation of toilet roll to an objet d'art.

Rosemary Shirley is an artist, writer and editor of *Leisure Centre*, an artists' zine.

The Caravan Gallery's approach to documenting everyday places, and the activities of the people who inhabit them, requires an adjustment in outlook, an attunement to the previously unnoticed, unremarked upon and ignored. However, this way of working does not simply focus on the minutiae of everyday life to the exclusion of everything else. It would be more accurate to say that The Caravan Gallery's photographs demonstrate a lack of differentiation between what is considered significant and insignificant. In this way their body of work records elements as diverse as the results of city council regeneration strategies to the recent boom in fried chicken take-aways and tanning salons. This approach to not only recording but also appreciating the everyday was advocated by French writer Georges Perec. In his essay *Approaches to What?*, written in 1973, Perec uses the term L'Infra-ordinaire (the Infra-ordinary) to describe the practice of attending to the particularities of everyday life which are neither exotic nor banal, the idea that we should observe what happens when nothing happens, as this is the texture of life as it is experienced. Perec describes exercises which can be used to attune ourselves to the infra-ordinary. He urges "describe what remains: that which we generally don't notice, which doesn't call attention to itself, which is of no importance; what happens when nothing happens, what passes when nothing passes except time, people, cars and clouds"[1].

This kind of attention to the everyday, however, does not produce everyday results. In the images presented by The Caravan Gallery the everyday is made strange, the familiar is shown to be unfamiliar. The absurdities, eccentricities and anomalies of location and behaviour that we had perhaps become numb to, rise to the surface, often resulting in laughter sparked by recognition.

Maxine is Unrealistic

Maxine has not thought this through, she's started too far over and now the long words don't quite fit on the wall properly. Maxine knows the rhyme off by heart, we get the impression that she has probably written it before, on a school bag or folder or her best friend Kelly's arm. It is even possible that on these previous occasions it wasn't Lynchie's name teamed with her own, but one of her earlier infatuations. However this fact does not necessarily negate the sentiment; perhaps we should applaud Maxine's optimism, if not her chosen method of public

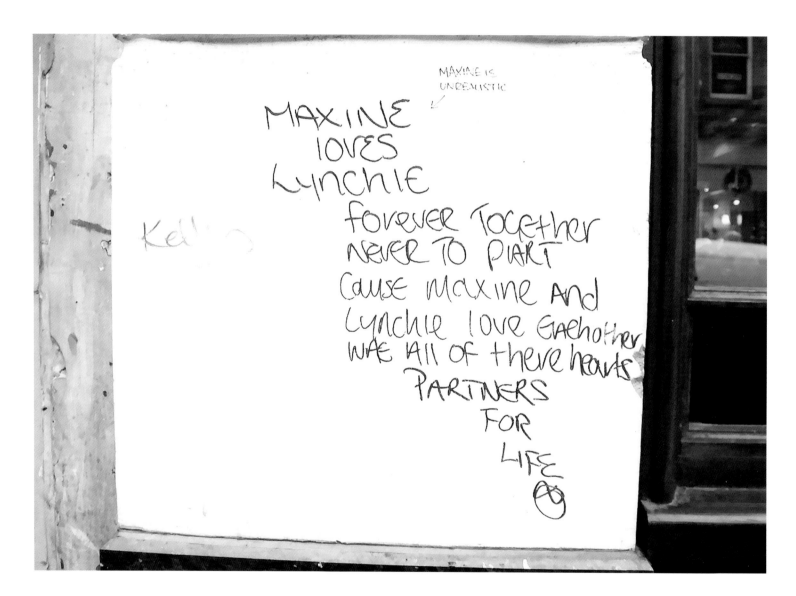

Maxine Is Unrealistic, Edinburgh

expression. Graffiti was amongst the subjects studied by Mass-Observation. Its more poetic members felt that such manifestations revealed the unconscious collective life of England, exposing hidden thoughts and dreams. This belief, influenced by Surrealism and the writings of Freud, sent observers into public toilets and telephone boxes to copy down the writing on the walls.

Mass-Observation was started in 1937 by poet and writer Charles Madge and anthropologist Tom Harrisson, together with surrealist artist Humphrey Jennings. To announce the movements beginning the founders placed a now renowned advert in the New Statesman calling for five thousand volunteer observers to report on phenomena such as:

Behaviour of people at war memorials,
Shouts and gestures of motorists,
The aspidistra cult,
Anthropology of football pools
Bathroom behaviour
Beards, armpits, eyebrows,
Anti-Semitism,
Distribution, diffusion and significance of the dirty joke,
Funerals and undertakers,
Female taboos about eating,
The private lives of midwives[2]

This all inclusive approach generated a unwieldy archive containing thousands of observations scribbled down on bits of paper and sent in by a committed team of observers. The archive also contains responses to questionnaires, one day diaries and file reports on particular subjects.

During their extensive travels around the British Isles over the past six years, The Caravan Gallery have amassed a similarly large collection numbering over sixty thousand images. An archive of such proportions presents obvious problems regarding use, display and categorisation; it takes on its own logic, its own rationale. This is perhaps most apparent in the artists' decision to reject the more traditional categories of geographical location or date order, instead electing to organise the images by subject matter. This move results in a bewildering array of digital folders with titles such as: balconies, bus shelters, churches-cum-cinemas, dead conifers, fun and happiness, hand-written notices, lewd graffiti, model railways, petrol stations (abandoned) and smut and innuendo. The Caravan Gallery share not only their love of eccentric subject matter with Mass-Observation but also their feeling for volume - the necessity of mass. Whether producing a book or an exhibition The Caravan Gallery are always involved in an unsatisfactory process of editing, as each image contains its own particularities, interest, humour or pathos and has its own place within the archive; they all need to be there. Volume often goes hand in hand with studies of the everyday, it is a generative process, one which mirrors the ceaselessness of the everyday itself.[3]

Can The Caravan Gallery's collection of images of Britain be transformed from a series of singularities into meaningful information about the way we live today? Do they provide evidence of a collective British identity? Is it possible to move from the micro to the macro, the particular to the general in this way? Perhaps these are not the right questions to ask of The Caravan Gallery's archive, because, like Mass-Observation, The Caravan Gallery operates outside and in between the quantitative scientific methods which yield so called representative results. Operating in this way something much more interesting is achieved, something perhaps best summed up by Mass-Observation themselves: "Mass-Observation has always assumed that its untrained observers would be subjective cameras. Each with his or her own distortion. They tell us not what society is like but what it looks like to them."[4]

A Traditional Cream Tea
Bird watching is a popular leisure activity, it is not unlike people watching (Tom Harrisson one of the founder members of Mass-Observation was an award winning ornithologist as well as an anthropologist). I am reliably informed that there is no such bird as a seagull, that it is in fact a generic name encompassing a myriad of different species of gull; however this does not change the fact that seagulls love cream teas almost as much as tourists do. It could be argued that watching seagulls scavenge cream teas, ice creams, pasties or chips, has become a kind of tradition

A Traditional Cream Tea, Tintagel

in itself, by virtue of its regularity if nothing else. However, it is not the kind of tradition that as tourists we are steered towards by guidebooks, brown signs or blue plaques. It is these very sights, the ones that happen while we're all supposed to be looking at something else, which The Caravan Gallery delight in attending to. They specialise in looking past the attraction, looking away from or behind the main event and, in so doing, often reveal that something much more interesting is happening elsewhere. Their images of people awkwardly wrestling oversized cuddly wild animals in Southsea, or photographs of garden gnomes cradled in a swing made entirely of Guinness cans in Newcastle are testament to the unimaginative nature of 'traditional' tourist information. Such leaflets and books are often subject to the censorious gaze of image conscious local government who, desperately trying to live up to slogans such as "Hampshire: Jane Austin Country", choose to endorse a 'heritage' which neglects the everyday or perhaps more transient contributions of its local residents.

In his book *The Art of Travel* Alain De Botton bemoans the tyranny of the guide-book and the empty experience of place which can result from a close adherence to its recommendations. He speaks of how a hierarchy of sights is constructed through the starring system often employed in such publications, the implication being that the tourists' interest should increase and decrease exponentially with the amount of stars awarded to the sight. Following this logic it is possible to intuit that where the guidebook is silent, awarding no stars and therefore no mention, the object or sight of interest is actually of no interest and should be ignored. This works to discourage the tourist from exercising their own curiosity and exploring places which offer genuine personal interest. De Botton subverts this system during a trip to Madrid by developing his own list of things he found interesting about the city which included "the under representation of vegetables in the Spanish diet...the long and noble-sounding surnames of ordinary citizens...the smallness of male feet and the attitude towards modern architecture in many newer districts of the city."[5] Through a similar process of looking away from the officially condoned attraction, The Caravan Gallery are able to subvert the culture of 'traditional English heritage' and create an alternative engagement with place, an engagement which could be considered to be more meaningful than any dictated by a guidebook.

The process of looking at the work of The Caravan Gallery is in some ways addictive, it is easy to find oneself moving from image to image looking for the next hit of laughter. However even though a large proportion of the work is undoubtedly comic, after this initial strike, the images can also go on to inspire responses such as wonder, pathos and dismay. Above all they make the familiar strange to us and in so doing initiate the viewer into a culture of re-noticing the everyday, of attending to the extraordinary ordinary.

References

1. Perec quoted in Ben Highmore (ed.), *The Everyday Life Reader* (London: Routledge, 2002), p176.
2. Angus Calder and Dorothy Sheridan (eds.), *Speak for Yourself a Mass-Observation Anthology 1937–1949* (Oxford: Oxford University Press, 1985), p.4.
3. The idea of the ceaselessness of everyday life is mentioned in Ben Highmore, *Everyday Life and Cultural Theory An Introduction* (London: Routledge, 2002), p.21.
4. Calder and Sheridan p.5
5. Alain De Botton, *The Art of Travel* (London: Penguin, 2003), p.116.

PLATES

Brighton

Padstow

Skegness

The Fens

Liverpool

Portsmouth

Jaywick Sands

Bristol

Hartlepool

Liverpool

Leeds

New Brighton

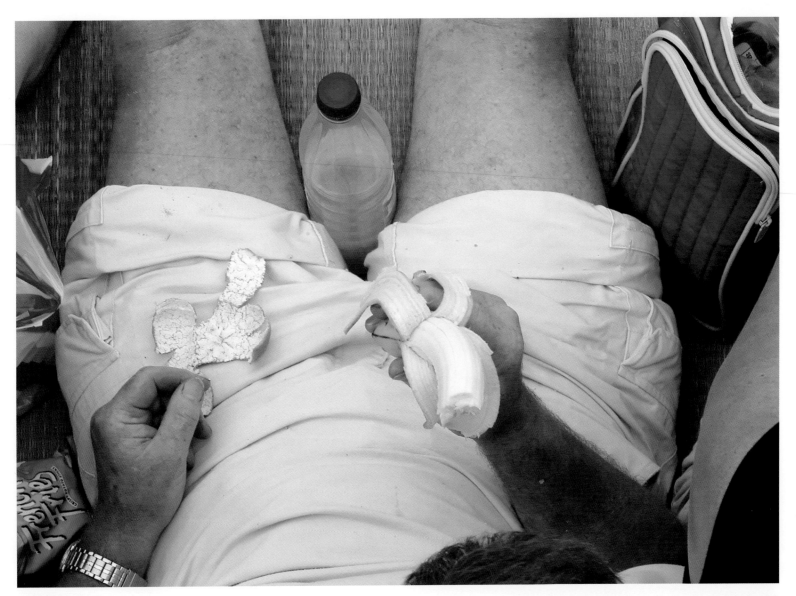

Perranporth

Bristol

Wolverhampton

JOB VACANCY

EXPERIENCED PASTY CRIMPER

Approx 4 hours a day
Mon - fri

Please leave your details here

Mevagissey

Nottingham

Blackpool

Herne Bay

Tintagel

Portsmouth

The Fens

New Brighton

Winchester

Southampton

Slough

Hunstanton

Fleetwood

New Brighton

Perranporth

Southsea

Everywhere

Arlesford

Edinburgh

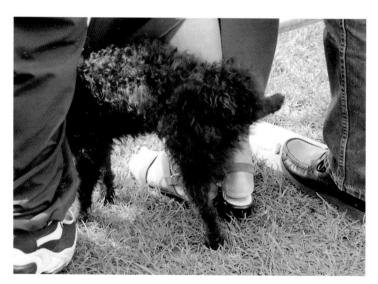

Southsea

Margate

Southsea

Fratton

Southsea

Liverpool

Portsmouth

Cambridge

Liverpool

Dungeness

Stow-on-the-Wold

Stow-on-the-Wold

Stow-on-the-Wold

Stow-on-the-Wold

Portsmouth

Bournemouth

Newquay

Hove

Southsea

Southsea

Leeds

Baldock

Thong's
3 Pair
£2.99
2 for £5

Newcastle & Gateshead

New daily service from Portsmouth fo

Portsmouth

Ipswich 2002

Ipswich 2005

Edinburgh

Blackpool

Maidstone

Sunderland

Ramsgate

Morecambe

Bournemouth

Morecambe

Kirkby

Toxteth

Fleetwood

Birmingham

Luxulyan

South Gare

Garstang

Wyre

Liverpool

Penwith

Canvey Island

Christchurch

Wallsend

Margate

Downham Market

Newcastle

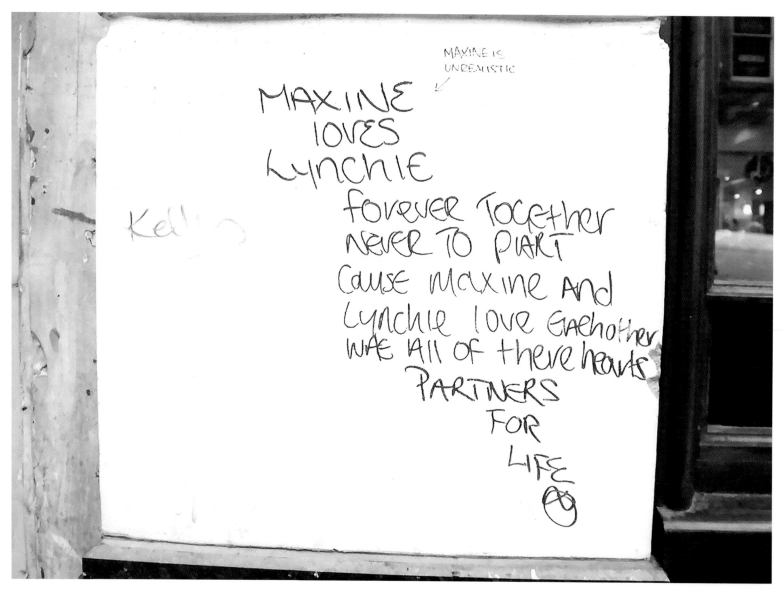

Edinburgh

London

THIS STONE HAS BEEN ERECTED
FOR THE COMMUNITY BY
TREVERBYN PARISH COUNCIL
TO CELEBRATE THE MILLENNIUM.
JANUARY 1ST 2000

Bugle

Belfast

West Howe

Mevagissey

Jaywick

Hackney

Slough

Bristol

Liverpool

Southampton

Slough

ENTURY
S.

PLEASE DON'T BE SHOCKED
BY THE PRICE OF ANTIQUES
AS YOU STAND IN YOUR £150
TRAINERS THAT ARE 6
MONTHS AWAY FROM THE
BIN.
thank you

Mevagissey

Land's End

Sheffield

The Tricorn, Portsmouth

Belfast

The Tricorn, Portsmouth

Hackney

Sunderland

Southampton

Newcastle

Norwich

Liverpool

Liverpool

London

Fratton

Seaton Carew   Clapton

Southwold

Skegness

Newport, Isle Of Wight

Liverpool

Mousehole

Nottingham

Southampton

Notting Hill

Portsmouth

Tintagel

Edinburgh

THE CARAVAN
GALLERY

The Caravan Gallery

The Caravan Gallery is a gallery in a caravan and visual arts project run by artists Jan Williams and Chris Teasdale who are on a mission to record the ordinary and extraordinary details of life in 21st century Britain. Eager to examine clichés and cultural trends, they are particularly drawn to absurd anomalies and curious juxtapositions, typical of places in transition and in the process of reinventing themselves.

Simultaneously seduced by and suspicious of the rose-tinted tones of tourist information brochures, and frustrated by their yawning omissions, Williams and Teasdale have set out to redress the balance by sidestepping the brown signs and interpretation boards to see what lies beyond.

The photographs in this publication have been taken over a 6 year period since the artists rescued a small mustard caravan from a life of obscurity on Hayling Island and gave it a new lease of life as a mobile exhibition space. They form the basis of a much larger exhibition, The Caravan Gallery's first retrospective as well as a highly subjective portrait of life in Britain.

The Caravan Gallery has travelled extensively around the country contributing to exhibitions, linking up with art galleries, street festivals, architecture events and conferences, documenting the way we live today as regeneration fever sweeps the land. In keeping with their view of the picture postcard as a historical document, they have produced over 160 to date and their first book, 'Welcome to Britain – a celebration of real life', was published in 2005.

Having appeared in around 100 locations from Cornwall to Scotland and more recently Northern Ireland, Williams and Teasdale are acutely aware that this is by no means a definitive survey and know that they will never run out of material as they continue to explore and revisit aspects of our extraordinarily diverse contemporary landscape.

www.thecaravangallery.co.uk

CREDITS

Artists' Acknowledgements

We would like to thank all who have taken an interest in our work and supported us over the years – family, friends, funders, facilitators and members of the public – you know who you are! Caravanning just wouldn't be the same without you.

Particular thanks must go to Joanne Bushnell and all at aspex for allowing us to ask the question *Is Britain Great?* – and indulge in a spot of indoor caravanning – in its swanky new premises at Gunwharf Quays, Portsmouth. We're very honoured!

Thanks also to Arts Council England, South East for supporting the show, to PPG Design & Print for sponsorship and general brilliance, to CHK Design for producing a catalogue we can be proud of, to Alistair Robinson and Rosemary Shirley for their insightful interpretation of our work and to Spectrum Photographic for printing and mounting rather a lot of photographs.

Special thanks

PPG Design and Print's sponsorship of *Is Britain Great? The Caravan Gallery UK Tour* exhibition and catalogue comes as a result of a close relationship with both the artists and aspex, and a real commitment to support the development of the cultural life of Portsmouth and those involved in art and design.

Phil Payter, Managing Director of PPG, established the company in 1980 after graduating from Portsmouth Art College where he studied illustration. Repositioning himself as a graphic designer he established a studio and gradually moved into print. 1998 saw the purchase of the first of three factories and the first press in the following year. The company is a family concern; stepfather Dave is the ambassador (or delivery driver), brother Carl is a finisher and sister Carolyn, the public face of the operation, is in Sales. Even *'Dogsbody'* Robin has an important role to play as company mascot.

PPG Design and Print prides itself on doing a good job and giving the best service. It delivers print to the high quality that artists and galleries demand and is always willing to give technical advice and support. aspex and The Caravan Gallery have each worked with the company for many years and thank Phil Payter and his team for their involvement and sponsorship.

Published by aspex on the occasion of the exhibition *Is Britain Great?*
The Caravan Gallery UK *Tour*, supported by Arts Council England, South East
and PPG Design & Print.

ISBN: 0-9550258-1-8

Reprinted by The Caravan Gallery in 2007.

Photography: The Caravan Gallery, Jan Williams and Chris Teasdale
www.thecaravangallery.co.uk

Design: CHK Design, Christian Küsters and Hannah Dumphy
www.chkdesign.com

Print: PPG Design & Print, Portsmouth
www.ppgdesignandprint.co.uk

The Aspex Visual Arts Trust is a registered charity, number 1007620, and is
financially supported by Portsmouth City Council and Arts Council England,
South East.

aspex
The Vulcan Building
Gunwharf Quays
Portsmouth PO1 3BF
T: +44 (0)23 9277 8080
E: info@aspex.org.uk
www.aspex.org.uk